Hitched & Happy:

An Ode to a Happy Marriage

Hitched & Happy:

An Ode to a Happy Marriage

Allyson Harris, Author

Allyson Harris

2019

Copyright © 2019 by Allyson Harris

All rights reserved. This book or any portion thereof may not be reproduced or used in any manner whatsoever without the express written permission of the publisher except for the use of brief quotations in a book review or scholarly journal.

First Printing: 2019

ISBN: 978-0-359-34239-6

Lulu Press, Inc.

627 Davis Drive, Suite 300

Morrisville, NC 27560

www.facebook.com/hitchedandhappy

A very special thank you to my husband, Ray. Thank you for encouraging me to write this. You have brought more to my life than I could have ever imagined. I have thoroughly enjoyed making our memories together and am anxiously awaiting the next chapters in our storybook.

To my mom, Diana, who taught me how to be a wife & mother.

To my mother-in-law, Juanita, who raised this wonderful man.

To my sister, Anita, who understands.

Preface

I'd be lying to you if I told you having a happy marriage was easy, far from it. There were several bumps, detours and everything else in the road along the way to us getting here. There are still challenges that we face regularly and I'd be a fool to think that there won't be any in the future. Could my marriage be better? Absolutely! My husband is far from perfect and I, perhaps, am even farther from it. I will never tell you that my marriage is perfect, but we are indeed happy.

My husband, Ray, and I have been married now for just over seven years. We beat the notorious seven year itch! Some may question what makes me qualified to speak on happy marriages after only seven years. Well, I'll say that I'm not speaking on all happy marriages. I'm speaking on mine. Additionally, I know a number of people that have been married for much longer than we have that aren't happy at all. The number of years has nothing to do with it.

I know that writing this will likely open us up to some ridicule, judgment and attacks. We won't focus on that.

This book is not about my husband and what he's doing to contribute to our happy marriage. This book is also not chocked full of bible verses and teachings. My husband and I aren't deeply religious. More importantly, this is not a self-help book on what you need to do to have a happy marriage. What it is, is an honest account of how I began to approach my marriage after recognizing some changes I needed to make in myself. It's about my journey — my efforts, my actions, my words. I am a regular person, I don't have a degree in Psychology or Sociology and haven't done years of research on marriages. I'm just me and probably a lot like you.

Hitched & Happy

Allyson Harris

Southern Girl

I come from a large family. I was born and raised in the 8th ward of New Orleans, LA. My mother was a housewife who later ventured into a home based daycare business. My father worked for the United States Postal Service and was a small business owner providing tax preparation and DJ services. We were a family of seven kids, five girls and two boys. I was number six and the last girl. Everyone knew whose kids we were. It wasn't at all uncommon to hear, 'that's Smitty's child.'

My parents had been together since they were in high school and had gotten married at a very young age. My dad would tell us the story of how he'd seen my mother at school and told his friends he would marry her before even having met her. She was a cheerleader and he was a nerd, an unlikely match. But somehow, they ended up together.

They had pet names for each other like most couples do, Dee and Bae. I don't remember them really arguing a lot in front of us. I also don't remember them being overly affectionate with each other either (or with us for that matter). I would see them give each other the requisite pecks on the lips but I don't recall hearing them say I love you to each other. It's funny how I say it to my mother every time I talk to her now but as a child, I don't remember ever hearing it said to me. I remember seeing them get dressed up to go out together for special occasions and seeing my mom get flowers sometimes — always red roses. My dad used to give her fine jewelry for all the important holidays. I used to love watching them dance together — hand dancing and two stepping. My dad had his this move where he would lift his knee to the side. We would mimic him and called his move 'the paw.'

My parents played the typical, traditional gender roles in the household. My mom was a home maker and what my dad said was pretty much the lay of the land. She did everything for him — washed, folded and ironed his clothes, packed his lunch, fixed his plate. He wouldn't even scrape his plate before leaving it in the sink or on the counter. It wasn't until we got older and she began working for herself that I saw things change in the house, where she began to have a say in what went on. It was small things like, getting cable television that she paid for. But also some pretty big things, like when she allowed me to start hanging out with friends (males included) and have an official boyfriend that could take me out on dates.

As I look back on it now, there was an interesting dynamic to our household. It seems that there was a defined barrier as it related to our interactions with our dad. We didn't spend a lot of time with him because he was frequently working. I don't particularly remember him teaching me to ride a bike or playing with us in the yard. We always had to be quiet when he was home so not to disturb him. Another specific example that sticks out to me is that we oftentimes ate dinner separately from him. We would eat in the den or kitchen and he and my mother would eat in the dining room. As an adult I can somewhat understand why that happened. I can imagine that my mother was probably trying to give my dad some time to come down from being at work all day. Sitting around the table with seven boisterous kids may have been too much to take after working 12 hours. Or, they were likely having discussions about things to which our little ears shouldn't be privy. Whatever the reason, the memory stuck with me.

I distinctly remember my dad's smell. When I would give him a hug after he returned home from work, he always smelled like a mix of liquor, sweat, the outdoors and metal — like loose change or keys. He would often stop at the union hall on his way home from work to have some drinks and play chess with his buddies. My dad carried tons of change in his pocket all the time. He would empty his pockets on the dining room table every evening and there'd be tons of coins just laying about. We would often steal coins from that table and sneak off to buy frozen cups or penny candy.

My mom is the type of woman whose lipstick always matched her nail polish and her purse, belt and shoes would match as well. She always wore makeup — not a full face with eyeshadow, but concealer, powder and eye liner. She would tell us things like 'leave something to the imagination' in reference to us wanting to wear revealing attire or say we looked like a 'lady of the night' if we tried to wear too much makeup. She always looked much younger than her age. Part of that was due to her coloring her hair but mostly because she had great skin. I've been told that I closely resemble her. I can only pray that I age as well as she.

She was never much of a drinker. While we always had a fully stocked bar, she just didn't partake. Interestingly, I didn't acquire this habit. But she definitely had a shopping problem. I remember her hiding the bags from my dad. There'd be bags stuffed everywhere. Sadly, I do seem to have acquired this problem myself.

Allyson Harris

She did not tolerate smart mouths and would be quick to give you a back hand if you got out of line. You couldn't roll your eyes, suck your teeth, raise your voice, slam a door or stomp off or you would feel her wrath. She was the primary disciplinarian because she was at home all of the time. Sometimes she'd threaten us with 'wait until your dad gets home' as if it was somehow worse than the punishment she'd impose.

As a young child, I didn't understand that times were hard. We seemed to always have what we needed and I had all the toys I could stand. But in today's standards, we'd probably be considered poor. I used to get excited about back-to-school shopping and my mom creating lay-aways at Kmart and Zayre for our underwear and book bags. I didn't really start to feel that things were different for us until I was in high school. That's when I started to notice everyone else wearing name brands and that the other girls had salon acquired hair styles. We didn't get to have the popular clothes and expensive shoes; we primarily shopped at the thrift store. I even borrowed sneakers from my a neighbor because my 'Immy-Jimmies' (off brand knock-offs) were just not cutting it in gym class. Oh the joy I felt when I purchased my first Esprit book bag with my own money after having worked my first summer job.

My dad worked a lot of hours, late nights and weekends to provide for all of us. When he'd work a lot of overtime he would take us out for Pizza Hut or McDonald's or we'd pick up a box of Popeye's Chicken and shrimp fried rice. I loved going for the ride to pick up the chicken! My mom was not the strongest cook. She was the canned goods and box queen (it's no wonder that I can't cook!). Some of the meals we suffered through! I still have nightmares from the Mac 'n cheese with fish sticks or tuna fish and spaghetti with cut up wieners. But she made a mean pot roast, could fry up some chicken and pork chops and made a great pot of red beans. It was a rarity for us to go to a fine or upscale dining establishment. It had to be for some special occasion. I do distinctly remember going to Ralph & Kacoo's in the French Quarter following my high school graduation.

We always shared bedrooms and at one point while in elementary school, I shared a bed with my sister. I still don't know how we managed to not kill each other with three girls in one room. And if you can believe it, there was no stealing of anyone's clothes or shoes, thanks in part to our age differences. But I wouldn't get my own room until I moved out on my own.

By the time I came around, there were no more family vacations. I saw an old picture of my family playing in a pool somewhere. I distinctly remember that picture because my dad wasn't wearing a shirt and I had never seen my dad without a shirt on. For me, Spring and Summer Break were just that, a break. It never even dawned on me that our family would go out of town on vacation. As children, we spent the summers going to the library, doing preparatory lessons and playing. I hadn't even heard of playing recreational sports. I wouldn't take a real vacation until I was in college. I didn't even bother asking to go on my senior trip in high school. I knew my parents couldn't afford it but they would never have allowed me to go anyway. None of my older siblings had gone on theirs. I remember sneaking off with some of my INROADs buddies to Houston in my freshmen year in college. I still don't know how I managed to pull that off. I can't even remember what lie I came up with to convince my parents that it was a legitimate trip. That was my first time ever leaving Louisiana.

Popularity escaped me in school. I wasn't in the band, choir or allowed to play sports. I was allowed to participate in the Future Business Leaders of America club and that was it. It would afford me the opportunity to participate in academic competitions and even ride in the Homecoming Parade my senior year which were pretty rewarding experiences. I had a very small group of friends that I connected with and remained close with throughout high school. After graduation, we all went our separate ways to different colleges and universities and simply grew apart. My family had moved a few times throughout my childhood so most of our friendships were with people that attended the same school. While we did have neighborhood friends, those relationships always ended when we moved.

In reality, it was too difficult to build lasting relationships outside of school. My parents were strict, we got our butts whipped on a regular basis, well into our teens. As I think about it, being punished really only meant you couldn't go outside because we weren't allowed to talk on the phone or hang out with friends outside of the home. Lord, I used to dream about going to Skate Country to hang out (even though I couldn't skate for shit)! We couldn't have a boyfriend or wear makeup. I remember being an early teen and riding the bus to the mall once with my sister and purchasing a fitted red tank top with a scalloped neckline. That was likely my first clothing purchase. Well, when I got home and proudly showed off my purchase, my dad took one look at that top and I was promptly made to return it. My dad was not too keen on me wearing a red tank top. You would have thought I was wearing nothing at all.

Allyson Harris

Even after finishing high school we still had a midnight curfew. You could trust that the chain lock would be secured promptly at midnight whether you were in or not. My mom used to say nothing good is happening after midnight and would say only a lady of the night would be out that late. And there was no such thing as trying to sneak in or out. The only other exit was in the basement which was my dad's man cave. He was always in there, well into the wee hours of the morning. This largely contributed to my decision to move out while in college.

I wasn't particularly close to my siblings growing up. While I would say that I've gotten closer to some of them as we've aged, I'm still not very close to them. Not as close as we could be or as close as I'd like. The age differences between us made it so I never seemed to be in the same school at the same time as they were. We just kind of grew up separately. But they say I was a tattle tale. They were always getting into something they didn't have any business doing. I wasn't going to get a whipping because of them. So, apparently I told on everybody. All the time. I vividly recall them stuffing me in the dryer as punishment one time.

As you read this, you probably think this all sounds really sad and might even feel a bit sorry for me. Don't. Sure, my childhood was seemingly rough but it wasn't all negative. I'm not the least bit ashamed of it. As I've aged, I recognize the lessons I learned from it. But I also have a ton of fond memories from growing up. I played with my siblings just like everyone else. Baby dolls, Barbie dolls, paper dolls. Who could color the best picture, which was always my sister Alicia. And we had quite the imagination. I remember using tomato carts and facial tissue boxes as cars for our dolls because there was no Barbie corvette. I loved playing outside, riding bikes, playing double dutch, hop-scotch, 1-2-3 red light, getting wet with the water hose. We would go outside seemingly as soon as the sun came up and wouldn't come back in until the street lights came on. Hell, I remember eating lunch outside in our yard on a blanket under a pecan tree and even taking naps outdoors. Even when it rained, we would sometimes play in it or sit on the porch swing waiting for it to stop.

We were a family that played board games together as well. I distinctly remember Sunday morning games at the dining room table with my dad. Word games from the newspaper, Backgammon, Dominoes, Life, Monopoly, Checkers, Pitty Pat, 21, War, Trouble, Sorry and, of course, UNO. We also had a RadioShack Intellivision video game and we could only play for a short period of time. That game was the epitome of slow!

Allyson Harris

I loved watching game shows and soap operas with my mom and old westerns and science fiction movies with my dad. I remember all of us kids watching prime time television together and not really being able to get engrossed in a tv show because of our strict 830pm bed time. My oldest brother was infamous for yelling, 'guess what time it is kiddies!' He couldn't wait for us to go to bed so he could hog the television. I still want to punch him in the face for that.

I have the best memories of big family dinners around the holidays. I loved visiting my grandmother and seeing all of my cousins. My grandmother made the best gumbo. And my parents would always make us dance for everyone. This is probably why I can't resist dancing every chance I get.

We had the best family tradition of going to my grandmother's house on Christmas Eve and singing Christmas carols while my aunt played the piano. We would drink hot chocolate and eat donuts while we would search for Santa's sleigh in the sky. I honor this tradition in my home now (although there is an adult version that hot chocolate now). We would wake up at the crack of dawn on Christmas morning to open our presents while we listened to old Christmas music, eat a big breakfast and watch the Macy's Christmas parade.

We had an annual Easter egg hunt at my grandmother's house. We would have our Thanksgiving dinners at my aunt's nursery. My dad would barbecue on the smallest grill imaginable for all the summer holidays while we played in the yard. We would watch my dad pop fireworks on all the appropriate holidays, giving us sparklers to hold while we sat on the porch. I remember my mom making egg nog on New Year's Eve and us sitting under blankets enjoying the fireworks show. As I recall these memories it brings a smile to my face. I would honestly say that my childhood was pretty damn good.

Allyson Harris

Love Life

I had done well enough in high school to secure early admission and a partial scholarship to attend Loyola University New Orleans. I was on top of the world. It was my father's alma mater. As a child I distinctly recollect saying that I would attend Loyola and become a Corporate Lawyer (I loved watching L.A. Law). I felt a tremendous amount of pride to be able to go to school there and I wanted nothing more than to make my dad proud. While attending school I held a full course load, worked a part-time retail job as well as did work-study and an on-campus part-time job. I had no time for leisure.

I didn't manage it well at all and lost my scholarship. I enjoyed skipping class entirely too much. I was about to drop out altogether but opted to secure student loans to finance my education. I didn't think about the long term implications of financing such a significant amount of money. I just didn't want to disappoint my parents. But I also didn't want to limit my career options by not getting my college degree.

I moved in to my first apartment in my sophomore year. I desperately needed my freedom. I had been fortunate enough to make an impression on my Admissions Counselor and her husband who let me rent their furnished studio for $250 a month. It was right on the streetcar line. I will never forget getting my first layaway at Kmart with a 19-inch television, iron and ironing board, bedding, pots, plates and utensils. I was terrified at being on my own but liberated at the same time. I remember having a housewarming party! Can you imagine? My new college buddies actually came through with gifts! I still have some of them. I didn't have a car yet so I was still catching the streetcar to and from work and school. I remember buying my weekly groceries at the neighborhood Walgreens. Frozen pizzas and hot pockets were my friends. No wonder my 'freshmen 15' was more like the 'freshmen fifty.'

I somehow managed to meet a guy that same year and we dated throughout the rest of our college careers. He was the preppy, frat boy type. A bit nerdy, wrote poetry. But I liked my guys smart. He was active in the Black Student Union and played rugby. He was amiable, the kind of guy you expected to go on and do great things. He introduced me to 2Pac, Pharcyde, Tribe Called

Quest, OutKast and Goodie Mob. He once took me to Atlanta for a weekend trip. He had a good family that welcomed me.

In our senior year, he proposed to me while I was at my work-study job in the pool hall. He'd hidden the ring on a stuffed rabbit's ear. I was over the moon. I had no idea that I was too young and immature to even think about being somebody's wife (neither did he, apparently). It seemed as if it was the natural progression for our relationship. We were living together and in our senior years in college. After college, of course we'd get married. Well, it didn't last. All I could talk about was that I was engaged and about our wedding plans. I must have been a nightmare to be around. I lost a good friend because of it.

That isn't why it didn't work out, though. I didn't trust him. I'd learned that he was basically the 'weed man' on campus. How did I not know that? How did I learn that from someone else and not him? If he would keep something like that from me, what else was he being deceitful about? Also, things were *off* at home. The phone would ring and when I'd answer, the caller would hang up. Or he'd tell me that he didn't want to go out and then he'd get a call and leave. I got really paranoid about it and couldn't move past it. So we ended it. He didn't want to marry someone who didn't trust him and he shouldn't. What I learned from that experience, besides needing to grow up a bit, was that I allowed myself to be consumed by my relationship. I didn't have my own identity. Even my 'friends' were his friends.

I pretty much became a recluse after that. I moved back to my parents' home in Gentilly. I literally slept on a loveseat in my parents' breakfast nook. Everything I owned (a 19 inch tv and my wardrobe) was cramped in that small space. Only my middle sister and younger brother were living at home at that time. I could have moved back into my old room with my sister but there was no way in hell I was going to do that. She'd had my nephew by then and he was a toddler. I would have to share the room with the both of them. No, ma'am. It would be impossible for me to do homework, study and sleep in that environment. So, on to the kitchen I went. I actually put a standing screen at the entryway to afford me some privacy.

I think this is when my relationship with my parents grew stronger. As a child, I think I naturally rejected what they had to say because it was always against what I wanted to hear. But as a young adult, they helped me when I was at my lowest point. They were there for me when no one else was. I began to actually talk with them and heed their wisdom nuggets.

It was during that time that my dad bought me my first car, a 1990 gray Pontiac Grand Am. My ex fiancé had taught me to drive and taken me to get my driver's license a year before. But since I moved back home I was back to catching the bus to get everywhere. I was carrying a full load at school and working three jobs, coming home well after midnight. It wasn't safe for a woman to be walking the streets of New Orleans late at night, alone. I was shocked that my dad did that for me. He hadn't bought any of my siblings before me a car. I don't know how he managed to afford it. The interior and exterior were in pristine condition. But I had to put it in park at stop lights to keep it from vibrating. The check engine light was always on. I despised that car but at the same time I was so deeply appreciative for it. It was all mine. It gave me that small bit of independence that I so desperately needed.

I finished my undergraduate program in December of that year. It was a tremendous accomplishment for me. Not only because I finished school but because I was able to do it whilst I was moving past my heartbreak and rebuilding my life. I promptly set about the business of getting a good job. I became laser focused on building my career and climbing the corporate ladder. I had been fortunate to have several internships throughout college that gave me a jumpstart at securing a great job fresh out of school.

I slowly began to find myself again and started to live a social life. I'd gained confidence in myself and found my identity. I finally moved out of my parents' kitchen and got an apartment in Metairie with a roommate. I got back into dating a little bit but nothing serious. I was mostly focused on having fun.

The next few years saw me hustling. I was working side jobs to help make ends meet. I had obtained decent, full-time HR jobs working at the big banks in the city and with a family owned hospitality conglomerate. They had good benefits but I was still making less than 30k a year. So I was always working part-time retail somewhere. I worked at Ann Taylor, Banana Republic, Cabana and even sold Avon for a spell. In 2000, I landed my dream job with Starwood Hotels at the W New Orleans. It was quite possibly the coolest place I'd ever seen. My first month on the job, they sent me to New York City for a week of training. I'd never even been on a plane before or been out of the southeast part of the United States. I was in hog heaven. I explored New York City all by myself, taking the subway and ferry to see everything that I could. I thoroughly enjoyed myself. That experience opened my eyes to a completely different life and I wanted all of it. The fear of the unknown was forever lost to me.

Allyson Harris

The dating scene hadn't improved much but I'd been in a handful of relationships. I'd even been proposed to twice more. Yes, twice. I know what you're thinking, what in the hell? How am I getting these men to propose to me? I have no idea, truly. I swear I am not the girl who cried engaged! I look at those situations in a few different ways: 1) thank God I didn't marry those people, 2) I wasn't ready (and neither were they), 3) I got caught up in the magic, the idea of getting married. I should have never said yes to begin with.

One of those guys treated me very well but I just couldn't see a future with him. I knew I wouldn't be happy in the long term. I felt that he would hold me back or he would later resent me for taking him out of his comfort zone. We were in a long distance relationship and we were both burning up the road back and forth to Memphis for the better part of a year. I had no real desire to move to Memphis. I couldn't see a trajectory for my hospitality career there. At the time, I was the HR Manager at the W New Orleans on Poydras. There was only The Peabody Hotel in Memphis that was a similar class hotel. I would be severely limiting my job options if I moved to Memphis. I had no interest in changing industries at that point in my career; I loved what I did for a living and the company that I worked for. He was in construction, so in my mind, he could easily find a job in New

Orleans. Well, jobs in New Orleans didn't pay as well as they did in Memphis so he would be giving up a lot to move there. Ultimately, I really didn't want to marry him. If I really wanted to, I should have been willing to make a temporary sacrifice. I wasn't. More importantly, there were other little things about him that I thought would eventually become too much for me to bear. He had some nasty habits. Well, I didn't manage that breakup maturely. I was supposed to go up and visit him one weekend and opted to go to Biloxi with a girlfriend instead. When I didn't show, he drove to New Orleans to find me. When he called me, I should have gone back and faced him but I didn't. I treated him like shit. It surely wasn't my best behavior and I'm certainly not proud of myself. I still can't believe I did that to him, he didn't deserve it.

The other guy didn't treat me so well and I can truly say it was probably my worst dating experience. He almost broke me. This was also a long distance situation. We'd dated in high school and I probably hadn't seen him since. And one day, while I was at work, he showed up at the hotel to chat with a friend who'd also gone to our high school. He found out that I worked there as well and asked to see me. When he walked into my office, it was like seeing a ghost. Well, long story short, we rekindled our little romance. I found myself running up to Georgia to see him every few weeks. We'd spend the New Year together. And then he went off to war. Before he left, he told me he wanted to marry me when he returned. While he was gone, we would write each other, I sent him care packages and he would call me periodically. We were making our little wedding plans while he was away. When he returned from his tour, we arranged for him to come to New Orleans for a weekend visit. But he never showed or called. It was like he disappeared into thin air. His number no longer worked and I had no idea of how to find him. And just like that, it was over.

With one, I think he loved me more than I loved him, if I even loved him at all. With the other, I think I was hoping to validate my prior involvement with him and maybe surprise a few people. Who knew that I was the one who would end up being surprised? I certainly should have, our high school fling hadn't ended well either.

Needless to say, dating had left me a tad bit weary. I was ready for a change. Something new. Anything new.

So, when I was 26, I took a job transfer to Hollywood, FL. As a child I never thought I'd leave my home town; there's just no place like New Orleans. And I was not running away from my past; I just wanted something else for my life. I felt like I was on a hamster wheel that would never stop. I felt like I would keep working side hustles to make ends meet and recycling bad relationships. Additionally, despite how much I loved my job and the company I worked for, I knew I wouldn't get promoted anytime soon because I legitimately needed more leadership experience. Moreover, I now had ambitions of one day moving to New York City.

So when the opportunity presented itself, I took it. And boy, did I have fun in sunny south Florida. I got myself in shape, enrolled in my masters program at NOVA Southeastern University and started dating online.

I met a handful of decent guys. I was enjoying the single life and learning true independence. While I could still call my parents if I needed something, it was different from being able to drive a few miles to their house every weekend, wash clothes, eat their food, raid their fridge and ask for money. But I would definitely say that I was homesick. South Florida just did not feel like home to me. If I recall correctly, I was flying back to New Orleans almost every other month. While it was certainly beautiful and fun, it was drastically different. I felt like a fish out of water. I couldn't find a church home or the right hair salon. I missed the change of seasons. I didn't feel that I could anchor there.

Allyson Harris

I can count on one hand how many times I went to the beach while living there. I loved driving over the inter-coastal and seeing the ocean every morning and I loved sneaking out to the oceanfront pool at the hotel where I worked, just to take in the sight of the ocean. But for some odd reason, I didn't hit up the beach regularly. When family and friends came to visit, it would be a top priority to visit the beach but back then I didn't grasp what a treat it was to just sit out there alone and listen to the waves. And while I feel that I did take the time to explore all the area had to offer, I found that I liked it; I just didn't love it.

Living in Hollywood helped me to grow up a bit and genuinely helped to boost my career but I still had a lot to learn. It was there that I mustered up the nerve to get my passport and go on my first international trip to Paris and London, all by my lonesome. I'll never forget the feeling of liberation of traveling alone. My mom thought I was crazy and was worried sick. I also went on my first cruise to the Bahamas with a new buddy from work. Lord, were my eyes opened to the single life aboard that Carnival Cruise ship!

I have some great memories from my time there and truly made some life long friends. But a short 14 months after uprooting my life and relocating to Hollywood, I found myself ready to move on. I ended up taking a promotional opportunity that landed me in my first Director level position in Atlanta, GA.

Allyson Harris

The 'List'

It was 2008 and I was 32 years old, living in Atlanta, GA. I was pretty sure Atlanta was where I wanted to establish my roots, so in 2004 I decided to buy my first home. I'd found an older two bedroom townhome in Norcross that was close enough to Buckhead and the Perimeter area where I was working at the time. It was move-in ready but needed some serious updating to make it more modern. But I didn't care about that. I owned my own home. I was so proud of myself for cleaning up my credit, saving up the money for the down payment and for doing it by myself. I was so excited, I was completely unpacked the same day I moved in. After I finished, I sat alone on my sofa, drinking a glass of wine, just cherishing the moment.

I had a very small circle of friends and was leading a pretty good life. I travelled for leisure pretty regularly, enjoyed going to the theatre and concerts as well as hitting up the club scene. I'd dated a handful of guys since moving to Atlanta four years prior. Most of the guys I dated, I met online. It was just easier for me because I truthfully had a lot of difficulty meeting guys. I wasn't exactly the approachable type if you'd met me out. And as an HR professional, I felt uncomfortable dating people that I worked with. I didn't want there to ever be a concern about a conflict of interest and I was too afraid that I'd end up having to terminate them. So that significantly limited my dating pool.

When I was 25, prior to leaving New Orleans, I made my first list. This list was of things I wanted to accomplish both personally and professionally by the time I turned 30 years old. As a result of making that list, I began traveling internationally at least once annually (something I still do to this day), got my masters degree, bought a home and obtained my PHR certification. So, needless to say, I'd personally seen the power of writing down your goals.

So, like most single women, I made my 'list' of desired attributes for a significant other. First on the list — I didn't have any kids so I knew I didn't want to date anyone with kids. In my mind, I didn't have kids, so neither should they. I didn't want to deal with 'baby mama drama,' having to share my time or worse, him being strapped for cash due to child support. Other than that, I have to admit that it was a fairly materialistic list. I wanted someone who owned a home, drove a nice car, was handsome, was financially stable, etc. As I think about it now, I'm almost positive there was nothing on that list about character or maturity (a clear indication of my deficiencies in those areas). I was admittedly very self-centered.

I think that something my father told me once, greatly contributed to my desired attributes in a significant other. My dad used to do my taxes for me. One year, he told me that if I continued my current trajectory that I wouldn't be able to find a man. Men would be too intimidated to date someone that made more money than them, were more established or held a higher position. I was flabbergasted. It was a punch in the gut, a slap in the face. The same man that had pushed me to attend college and seek a burgeoning career was now telling me to slow down to improve my chances of finding a husband?! What the fuck?! That just couldn't be right. I wasn't even making that much money at the time, but it clearly must have been more than he was making. What my dad was really telling me was that a woman's financial independence meant that she didn't need a man. He was spouting his traditional and antiquated views to me as if they were right. I completely rejected that thinking and sought out to prove him wrong. There had to be men that valued a woman that made her own money and was successful. And I surely wasn't going to hold myself back out of fear that I wouldn't find a man that could handle my independence. If such a man existed that was emasculated by my salary and position, then he just simply wasn't the man for me. I think this may have fostered in me an attitude, an arrogance towards men. Hence, my list.

But up until that point, I'd had a decent dating experience. I can honestly say that there were only a couple of bad situations, but I was able to move past them. I didn't subscribe to the 'all men are dogs' mantra. I had dated a guy who didn't have a car, did the long distance thing, dated someone that had a kid, dated a 'rough neck,' etc. But I had also met several very nice guys who possessed most of the attributes I'd listed. They just weren't the right fit for me. I'd had fun but nothing had gotten too serious for more than five years. Could that have been because my list was too 'basic' and lacked the substance of true human qualities? Probably. Did I still have some growing up to do before I was ready for a serious relationship? You bet, but you couldn't tell me that.

I met Ray online in February that year and we had been dating a few months. He'd sent me an instant message through Yahoo Messenger. I'm still a little perplexed by this because I honestly don't recall ever setting up a profile on Yahoo Personals. I had profiles on match.com, Eharmony, Black People Meet, Black People Connection, but not Yahoo

Personals. What attracted me to him initially was his eyes. His profile pic was of him sitting on the couch with this 'come hither' look. But also, we'd exchanged a ton of instant messages, emails and texts and he was clearly intelligent. I liked that he was articulate, could spell and put together a proper sentence. Don't judge me! I knew I needed to be with someone who would be able to hold their own in a professional environment but also someone with whom I could have an intelligent conversation. He was in to politics, music and nature and was up on current events. So, we agreed to meet in person. We had our first date at Taco Mac on Holcomb Bridge Road. I don't think I had ever been to a Taco Mac before. It was his favorite spot for two reasons, beer and wings. Two things that I couldn't care less about, hence my never having been there. But I agreed to meet him anyway. It was just a regular date, nothing fancy. Truthfully, I'd been on better first dates. There was not a ton of chemistry there but there was definitely something about him that made me want to get to know him a little better.

He was different than just about everyone that I'd dated prior. While I can't say that I had a type, he didn't really check off the things I had on my 'list.' He didn't own a home, he drove an old Dodge Ram and wasn't independently wealthy. He was several years older than me and wasn't really in to 'going out.' He had two school aged kids. He spent every other weekend with his youngest son (read: that's a weekend I wouldn't get to spend with him).

Ray had been raised in a single parent household and hadn't met his father until he was an adult. He was a middle chid with two sisters. His family was close knit and did just about everything together. As a child, he had been raised in a similar economic environment as me. Despite not having lived in Greenville since he was college aged, he still had strong ties to his community.

He'd attended Morehouse College in Atlanta, GA and left in his senior year in order to better provide for his newborn daughter, taking her to live in Charlotte, NC with his mother. He later relocated back to Atlanta, leaving his young daughter to be raised by his mother. As he settled into bachelor life and got established here in Atlanta, things were going well for him. He was finding his footing. When his son came along, he sought about trying to do the right thing. And as we all know, things don't always work out and he moved on from it.

I tell you these few factoids about Ray's background because they help tell the story about who he is and why he is the way he is. These few events very much shaped how he approaches everything in life.

Everything with him was different; but more importantly, HOW we dated was different. I was accustomed to doing the same date-type things as most people — movies, dinner, shows, etc. But we would ride bikes together, go on hikes, fishing. We even went to Pull-A-Part together (he was restoring a Cutlass at the time). I'd never done any of those things with anybody, nor did I have it in my mind to want to. We did all of the 'normal' stuff too but I found myself really appreciating these new experiences with him. Some of you may be reading this and equating our dating excursions to his being cheap. Well, truth is, he didn't have a lot of money but he wanted to spend time with me, so he made a way. My dating experience with Ray opened my eyes to what was really important — the quality of the time we were spending together versus what activity we were doing together. I got to see the real him and he was a real gem.

I offered to have him spend Easter Sunday with my family that year because he wasn't going up to Greenville to be with his family and he accepted. Let me tell you, he made himself quite comfortable at my folks' house. My parents liked him immediately. My sisters gave him a nickname, 'Too Loose,' because that mouth of his did not take a holiday. He was all too ready with his sarcasm and clever comebacks. He fit right in with the Smith clan. And as I dropped him off at his car, we shared our first kiss.

We became official shortly after that when he asked me to be his girlfriend. We hadn't even slept together at that point. My sister would call me a prude but I didn't want to muddy the waters with sexual tension and be blinded by lust before really getting to know him. What can I say? Call me old fashioned.

Then he introduced me to his adorable son. We met for lunch at Atlantic Grill in Atlantic Station. His son was still small enough to be in a stroller. He sat across from me and stared at me with smiling eyes the entire time. There would be a few more occasions where we got to hang out together and we undoubtedly hit it off. He was unquestionably the sweetest kid.

Then things changed. He was doing a lot of business traveling. I wasn't getting the attention I felt I deserved (Read: I was being selfish and immature). Not only could he not see me as much but he couldn't really talk to me either. The nature of his business travel did not afford him the luxury to be chatting on the phone. When he was at home, he was exhausted from traveling. This was for the birds! I'm sure he grew sick of me naggingly texting him all the time. But it was no longer working out for me. So one night after he returned from a business trip, I told him so and we ended it. I wanted someone who was going to be around. I honestly never thought I'd see him again.

Later on, I was catching up with an old friend from back home and she introduced me to the book, *The Secret*. It was all about the law of attraction. Go ahead and roll your eyes now. I know most of you have probably heard of it. My friend claimed that it changed her life. Having personally seen the positives changes in her life for myself, I figured why not give it a read? It couldn't hurt. So, I read it and digested it. It was short, an easy read, pretty repetitive. But I took a lot from that reading. Most importantly, the concepts of having a positive outlook and making positive affirmations truly resonated with me. To this day, I go back to these concepts in every aspect of my life. I *TRY* to get my husband grounded in it as well, as he can be a 'Negative Nelly' sometimes— but he's still a work in progress. When I read that book I had no idea that those very concepts would take us from the early stages of our relationship to our engagement to our now happy marriage.

I strongly believe in writing down what you want and speaking desires into fruition. I did this before I read *The Secret*. Any churchgoer can preach about this. I was already applying that methodology to every aspect of my life. Just as in the *Bible*, *The Secret* also taught me that faith without works is dead. You have to be worthy and ready to receive what you are asking for or you'll muck it up. You may get everything that you ask for and something's still wrong, it still doesn't work out. What's the common denominator, the constant in those situations? You.

I took a good look at the list of things I'd said I wanted in a significant other. I had to think about why I really wanted those superficial things. I had been in happy dating situations without having those materialistic things. What was truly important? I then took a good, long, hard look at myself in the mirror and I asked myself some questions. Is the person I'm manifesting going to want me as I am? What am I bringing to the table? Did I think that because I didn't have kids and was independent that that somehow made me a 'catch?' And most importantly, what did I need to work on? NOBODY is perfect, but surely striving for betterment is a good thing. Why did my past relationships fail? Was it truly all the guy's fault? Was I jealous? Petty? Needy? Vindictive? Immature? I had been all of those things and more at some point. Was I an unhappy person? Did I think that being in a relationship would make me happy? Did my happiness really rest on my having someone special in my life? That couldn't be right. I'd been pretty damn happy as a single woman. I was living a great life but I wanted something more. I wanted someone to share my happiness with.

What I wanted, not needed, was a companion to complement my life. Someone who could teach me something, help me grow and who wanted to build something together. So, I threw that damn list out and started a new one with the aforementioned considerations at the forefront. Gone were the superficialities. When I was done and looked at it, I kept seeing Ray. You're probably thinking that I was just lonely and missed having him around. Maybe, but that didn't change who he was and what I wanted in a mate. Furthermore, he hadn't mistreated me. I was at fault for where we stood because of my selfishness and immaturity. I had come to the realization that some things that you want, may not come in the exact package you want. You may get surprised with a gift that's a little (or a lot) different than what you envisioned but you need to be able to recognize it's a gift all the same.

A month or so later, I humbled myself and called him. I asked if he would be open to seeing me. I had tickets to *The Color Purple* at The Fox and wanted him to come with me. Thankfully, he agreed. I stuffed my big behind in the sexiest dress I could find and showed up. I was nervous as all hell and he was too. It was awkward to meet up again due to how we'd ended things and the fact that we hadn't really spoken to each other since. I was just hoping to restart the connection. Maybe it would work out, maybe it wouldn't but I had to try. So I made my apologies and we started over, focused on getting reacquainted.

Allyson Harris

Turn of Events

After a short while, he moved into my two bedroom townhome. Lord, did this man have a lot of stuff. To this day he still has more clothes and shoes than me. I remember helping him pack up his apartment. He still had clothes he'd worn in college and hadn't worn since. He had been out of college almost 20 years! He ended up putting a lot of his items in storage because there really was no room for anything.

I already had a full house of furniture, most of which was fairly new as I'd bought all new furniture when I moved to Atlanta. They were pieces that I adored and had spent good money for. I was not even thinking about parting with any of them. He was lucky to get a closet and dresser in the guest room. He made it work but I don't think he really felt like it was his home too because nothing had his 'stamp' on it.

And my furniture lacked functionality, it wasn't meant for lounging. The living room set didn't even have arms. When I wanted to lounge around, I'd get in the bed. I didn't watch much television (I didn't even have one in my bedroom) or entertaining so I didn't select a living room set with that in mind. The living room was meant to be more of a sitting room. The tv was an old 32 inch box television set. That thing was huge and unbelievably heavy. I wasn't bothering with it. He, on the other hand, is a tv junkie! This man watches any and everything that comes on the tube. As soon as he walks in, he reaches for the remote and can be found asleep in front of the tv most nights (I swear it's his happy place). Later on, we would acquire a living room set, large flat screen tv and tv stand together. Those purchases were only made because of him. I still have heartburn over getting rid of my wooden tv cabinet! But making those purchases helped him to feel a bit more welcome, like it was his home too.

    I hadn't lived with a guy, or anybody for that matter, since I was college aged. This was a huge adjustment for me. If I wanted him to feel comfortable, I had to come to grips with the fact that he needed space for his things. He needed privacy and alone time. I also had to be more diligent about cleaning up around the house. I was certainly no neat freak but I noticed that I paid extra close attention to his things being strewn around. Then there was the cooking. Before he moved in, I cooked, but it was a rare occasion. I get no enjoyment out of it and frankly it can be a lot of work with the prepping and clean up. Before he moved in, I was going out probably four to five nights a week and when I wasn't going out, I was getting junk food. That just wasn't going to work anymore. So I called on my childhood memories of the basic dinners my mom used to cook to guide me. Lord, we ate way too much spaghetti with meat sauce and too many one-skillet meals!

Then, of course, an unexpected thing happened. It seems like not very long after Ray moved in with me, I don't recall exactly how much time had passed, his son came to live with us. Up until then, Ray was driving to Greenville, SC to see him every other weekend. We'd talked about the possibility of his son coming to live with us but I honestly wasn't expecting that to happen for several years. I anticipated that he would come when he was a teenager, but he was in kindergarten. Supposedly, it was because his mother wanted him to spend more time with his father. I'd be lying if I said I didn't think there were other ulterior motives. But I'm not even sure she knew I existed at that point. But none of it mattered. While it was certainly unexpected, I never considered not allowing it. Oh, I surely bitched about it, a lot. But in my eyes, I agreed that Ray needed to spend more time with his son. I couldn't help but think that it would be less stressful on him by not having to go up and down the road every other weekend. And I knew he wanted custody of him. I wasn't that naive to think that it wouldn't impact our relationship quite a bit, but I couldn't fathom at the time that it would be in more ways than I could name or even register. But how could I be selfish and say no?

But I knew nothing about raising a child!!! Please believe me when I tell you I didn't even know where to begin. As a teenager, I had babysat my nieces and nephews on occasion but that was completely different. I didn't know the first thing to do to prepare for this new reality. I told myself I was a grown up, I'll figure it out just like everyone else does. I prepared the guest room and tried to get my mind right. I figured I would just do what my mom did and pray that it would all turn out alright. And we settled into our new family life. He started at his new elementary school and quickly made friends in the subdivision. It was like he didn't even miss a beat. He made it fairly easy for me because he was, quite simply, an easy child. So cute and bright.

Now, I already told you about my upbringing. There was good reason for that. This is where the differences between Ray and I started to really show themselves. I had been raised in a strict household. You didn't talk back, you didn't have a choice or an opinion. My parents didn't coddle us. There was a parent (an authority figure) and a child — you would do best to know your place because you'd be quickly reminded should you forget. Is that right or wrong? Can't say; it is what it is. But, of course, this played out in the interactions with our son.

I would describe Ray's parenting style as very 'hands off.' He is definitely not a helicopter parent. He affords his son freedom and privacy. I didn't have privacy as a child, didn't even know what it was. We didn't even have doors to our rooms. He trusts that his son will always do the right thing and wants to give him the opportunity to do it. He would ask him what he wanted!! WHAT !@#$#%$#@?? I grew up in a household that you didn't get options, you got what you got. Whether it was food, clothes, toys, activities or whatever. Nobody asked me what I wanted, ever. Needless to say, this freaked me out! Did this have to do with how he was raised? Maybe. He has certainly described incidents from his childhood that left my jaw hanging. He was afforded much more freedom than I was. It was likely due to his being male. But nevertheless, I accepted that we had different parenting styles and that, for the most part, I had to honor his wishes with how he wanted to rear his son. But it wasn't a situation where he asked me not to engage with or discipline him. It was quite the contrary. Unfortunately, I quickly became the disciplinarian in the relationship.

I had to come to the realization that this child had primarily been raised by someone else for the past five years. He was accustomed to seeing his father every other weekend and for two weeks during the summer. When he saw his father, they mostly ate junk food and he often got new stuff. All fun and games, right? And here I was, with all my rules, home cooked meals and shit. While he and I surely got along well together, I had to be mindful of a lot and check myself. I didn't want to make an enemy of this child. I wanted him to feel at home, that he was in a place of love. But I also didn't want him to run our house, I had to set boundaries and establish routines in order for this to work. I. CANNOT. HAVE. CHAOS. I'd never experienced having to balance a full time job, a child's school and sleeping schedule with having to prepare appropriate meals at appropriate meal times. We had to learn his eating habits and idiosyncrasies on our own. There was no toolkit provided. If I didn't approach this mindfully, it could have been a complete disaster. On top of all of that, I also had to be careful not to give the impression that I was trying to replace his mother.

But things were actually working. We did a lot together. He and I became really close. He would snuggle up to me on the sofa or when I read him a story at bedtime. During this time, his mother would still see him but only twice a month on the weekends. He was so young that I knew he still needed that mothering and I filled that void. One weekend, he made an unexpected comment to me, 'my mom said you need to have your own child.' Now I know children repeat what they hear and that he was probably very confused about me. But baby, it took everything in me not to respond back with 'tell your mom to go fuck herself!' It was apparent that his mother felt that I was stepping on her turf. Well, when she put him on MY turf she had to deal with everything that came along with that. Due to his father traveling, I spent a lot of time with him. I never told him he had to call me mom or anything. He never has, still doesn't. But I never wanted him to feel that he wasn't wanted. He should never feel neglected or that the issues between his parents were his fault. And since he was in my care, he would be treated as if he was my child. As a parent, you would think that one would be thankful for that.

Now something you don't know is that I knew by this time in my life that I really didn't want to have any children of my own. I used to think I wanted kids. When I was much younger, college aged, I remember saying to myself that I wanted to have kids by the time I was 25. Ha! That time had long come and gone. If I'm completely honest, I've never felt the pangs of motherhood or had baby fever. I've never seen or held a baby and said to myself, I want one! Sure, who doesn't melt when they encounter an adorable baby? I think baby clothes and shoes are the cutest things ever. I love to buy them, but for other people. I've never felt that I was missing out on something or was a failure as a woman. Maybe it was selfishness, maybe it was my upbringing or maybe it was watching so many people that were close to me struggle with parenthood. Maybe it was all of those things or none of them. I really can't say. I just know that at that time in my life (and to this day), I couldn't see myself ever taking that path.

So, no, I don't have fertility problems (as far as I know). I just don't have the desire for a 'mini me' or the need to create another human being so I will have someone to take care of me in my old age or because I felt it was my duty as a woman to procreate. And please don't take my statements as me judging anyone that has those reasons. They are your reasons and you are entitled to them, they just are not mine. I wasn't going to have kids just because I could or because everybody else thinks I should have given Ray a child. He's got two. He's good.

Ray and I talked about my not wanting to have kids when we initially met. I don't think he believed me. He also told me that he really didn't want anymore kids, and I was totally fine with that. Besides, Ray's old ass sperm needed to stay where they were. Would I have felt differently if we were younger and he didn't already have kids? Not likely. Anybody who knows me well, knows that I'm just really not a kid-type person.

Am I telling you this because I think that my not having a child of my own made me approach this situation so willingly? I don't think so. Seriously, what was I supposed to do? Was I supposed to say no, he couldn't come to live with us? Was I supposed to end my relationship with Ray because of this? I feel that this situation was set before me for some reason. Whatever that reason was, I was going to do what I felt was right and do it to the best of my ability.

I knew he would struggle with the fact that his parents weren't together and figuring out my role in his life. There's no telling what he was being told about me and his father or what he thought about our relationship. I couldn't focus on that or it would drive me crazy. But what I could do was make him feel at home.

We've learned to ignore the things we hear about what's been said about us. Nothing can be done about it. It doesn't make sense to have a confrontation about it. What would that gain? We rest on knowing that we are doing all that we need to do and trust in that. The only opinion that matters is our son's. He may not appreciate or understand the totality of the situation now, hopefully he will as he ages.

One weekend sometime later that year, we drove up to tailgate at a Clemson Football game. Ray left me at the stadium so he could pick up something and came back with his mother. Now why he chose not to tell me he was bringing her along is beyond me. When he pulled up, I immediately knew it was her because he looks just like her. I swear I almost shat myself. At this point in our relationship, I hadn't met his mother yet. I had no idea that he was ready to do that. While he had already met my parents and siblings, this was very different. For some reason, I always introduced guys to my family early in a relationship. I guess it may have been for their approval, I can't say with 100% surety. He would later tell me that he didn't warn me because he wanted me to act naturally. Needless to say, I am sure I was as awkward as could be. I'm an introvert, so naturally I'm always uncomfortable meeting new people.

Let's just say I didn't walk away from that interaction with the best feeling about my first impression on his mother. I'm sure there was a bit of resentment towards me because when I came along, Ray started spending a lot less time in Greenville. He was building his life in Atlanta. I'm also guessing that there was probably a need for her to be protective of him given all he'd recently been through. She'd even told me in that first encounter — and I quote — 'I don't want anymore grandkids.' I was speechless. I could have let my 'New Orleans' come out but how does one even respond to that without being disrespectful? We weren't even talking about kids at the time, she said it completely out of the blue. The damage was done. That certainly structured how I would interact with her going forward. Years later we would laugh about that and she told me that she was only joking but I still can't help but wonder what led her to say that to me. I know I couldn't possibly have been giving off this 'put a baby in me' vibe. But it took a long time for us to build rapport with each other. I don't think there was even a minuscule level of comfort between us until well after Ray and I were married. When we got married, she even made the comment to me that we'd better not get divorced.

There would be a lot of other interactions with his family before we got married. Birthdays, tailgates and holidays saw us frequently driving north to Greenville. He showed me around his hometown and introduced me around. It seemed like his relationship with his immediate family was similar to mine. Not that they'd grown up separately but that he was sort of an outsider in a close-knit family. The reasons behind it could range from disapproval of his decisions regarding his kids or the fact that he chose not to live in Greenville or due to a dislike for me. Who knows? Maybe I'm imagining it all. But I know that he tried to make sure I was welcomed into his family as I did with mine.

I really got to see the good in Ray one evening after we attended his friend's wedding in Macon. I became ill like I've never experienced before in my adult life. I had no idea what was wrong with me, I was completely out of it. Ray took me to urgent care and later followed the ambulance to the hospital. He called my siblings to inform them that I was hospitalized. And he looked after me when we returned home. Turns out that I had some type of viral infection that caused a double ear infection and vertigo. Of course I didn't know at the time that there would be a few more incidents where he would need to do that for me. But following that particular experience, I felt comfortable knowing that I could trust him to take care of me if needed.

Allyson Harris

A New Chapter

Ray and I took a vacation to San Juan, Puerto Rico in July of 2010. It was an awesome experience and time away from it all, for the both of us. The past year had been crazy with us adjusting to having our son with us the majority of the time. I'm still amazed we were able to manage to take the trip at all. We visited the beautiful El Yunque Rainforest, walked the lovely streets of Old San Juan and drove to all of the lovely beaches of Vieques. On the last day of our trip, while we were enjoying the last few moments before heading to the airport, he proposed. I was sitting on the rocks in the secluded area at Condado Beach, overlooking the ocean. It was the most beautiful and majestic place he could have chosen. There was no one else around and nothing to see but crashing waves and blue sky. He was visibly nervous and fumbling with the ring in his pocket so he wouldn't drop it. We had bought the ring together so I knew he was going to propose at some point. But it meant a lot to me that he wanted to do it right and try and make it special, memorable. He didn't have to do that. It says a lot about him, what marriage meant to him and how he truly felt about me. I was beaming like a Cheshire cat all the way home. To top it all off, he would later surprise me with a photo book capturing the whole trip and telling a pictorial story of the engagement. I mean, come on! Isn't he the best?

I didn't tell my parents right away but we promptly made a quick trip up to Hiram to see them upon our return to Atlanta. They'd relocated to the area after Hurricane Katrina. Ray asked to speak to my dad privately and he officially asked for his blessing to take my hand in marriage. It was truly sweet. My parents already adored him. They were elated. I would be remiss if I didn't share that my mother reminds me of Mrs. Bennett from *Pride and Prejudice* with her desire to marry off her five daughters.

After we got engaged, everything changed. We didn't do pre-marital counseling and honestly should have. I know now that we needed to have larger discussions about how we would handle finances, raising his son and get deeper about the expectations we had for each other. I assumed we were mature enough to figure it out on our own and we would be ok. I learned pretty quickly, I couldn't have been more wrong. While we had been living together and had had some conversations about the future, we needed to have some other dirty, uncomfortable talks to ensure we were really on the same page about some other things. We needed guidance on how to effectively communicate with each other. We could have avoided a lot of unnecessary headaches.

Within a few months, we started looking for a house together whilst wedding planning. This was not part of the plan. I happened to be driving through our neighborhood and saw a white Cape Cod style home for sale. I called the realtor and Ray and I went to see it. That's how it all started. We hadn't done any of the pre-approvals or even sat down to talk about what we were looking for in a house let alone that we were ready to buy one. As you can see, I can be a bit impulsive. We did all of the pre-approvals after we saw that first house. We agreed on our must-haves and began the search.

We looked at what felt like a million houses. We put in so many miles driving around Norcross, Peachtree Corners, Lawrenceville, Duluth, Snellville. Ugh! It was unbelievably exhausting and disheartening. Ray was getting fed up. But the townhouse was too small with all three of us and a dog. We needed more space.

My boss at the time recommended that we look in the Suwanee area. I had never even heard of Suwanee. Prior to her moving to East Cobb, she'd lived in Suwanee and had nothing but good things to say about the area. It turns out that Suwanee had been rated the best place to live the year prior. So, why not at least check it out? Our realtor hadn't taken us to the area because it was a bit farther out than we requested but we asked her to expand the search to include it. She took us to see two houses in that area. Before we got to our house, the very last one we'd see, Ray said if we don't like this one, we are going to stop the search. Well, this one spoke to something in us and we went back to look at it again the same day. We put an offer in that night. It was bigger than we needed but it checked most of the boxes. It needed some updating to make it ours and more modern but it was certainly move-in ready. It was a mile from a library and golf course, across from an aquatic center, walking trails and neighborhood park and there was a community pool and clubhouse. The high school and elementary school were reputable and basically in our backyard. It was close enough to the interstate. It would be a great first family home and a great place to raise a kid. It would allow us to provide our son with opportunities and experiences that we didn't have as children.

When we put an offer in, we were met with nothing but adversity and had actually been told that we didn't get the house, three times. The third time was in the same week of the closing, literally days before we were scheduled to close. I was about to lose my mind. But thankfully, it all worked out in the end. Our son left on Friday for a weekend with his mother and came back to a new home on Sunday.

We closed on our house at 4:30pm, Friday, October 29th and moved in October 31st. We needed to get the townhouse rented out ASAP. We couldn't afford to carry two house notes. When we got the keys, we immediately drove up to do a walk-through and take note of what we needed right away. We stood in our big, empty house and looked at each other, just smiling. We'd done it. It was so surreal.

We had been packing the townhouse up for months but never communicated to anyone that we were officially moving. I had spoken it into fruition that we were moving and was planning accordingly but we didn't want to get too far ahead of ourselves. I didn't want the questions of where and when because we honestly didn't know. We'd put in offers on another house that hadn't worked out and had gotten three rejections on this house so we kept things under wraps for the time being.

At this point, Ray had communicated to his ex that we were taking our relationship to the next level and getting married. I was told the response was, "I don't want him calling her mom!" Now, I had met her before and we were cordial but that was it. After we moved in to our new home, she decided to relocate to Atlanta, I believe it was literally within the month. We were told it was under the guise of her needing to spend more time with her son. That could have been completely legitimate but what a coincidence that this need arose right after we got engaged and bought a house. But it was what it was. It didn't matter what her reasons were. I didn't like the idea of having to deal with her more frequently but there was absolutely nothing I could do about it. I tried to look at the bright side because it could only benefit our son to spend equal time with both of his parents, right?

Part of my thinking on that was a bit selfish, too. I strongly believed that a successful marriage was largely dependent on the couple building a strong foundation before introducing kids into the marriage. Well, we were already starting off with a deficit there. Splitting custody would allow us some time to reconnect with each other and focus on our relationship as a couple. I don't think anyone would argue that couple time in a marriage is important. I've heard a million stories about how some couples throw all of their time and efforts into their kids and when the kids grow up, there isn't anything left of the marriage. The couples have grown apart and are strangers and they ultimately end up divorcing. I didn't want that for my marriage so I embraced this new arrangement and really tried to see it as a positive.

We had opted to do a destination wedding. I had no expectation of my parents paying for anything. I knew that they couldn't afford it and to be honest, if they could, that meant we would have to respect their wishes on a lot of things. Truth is, as a child I always dreamt of getting married in New Orleans at Holy Name of Jesus Church or St. Louis Cathedral and having a horse drawn carriage, reception at Southern Oaks Plantation, complete with second line band, etc. The reality was, that dream was quite expensive. We'd just bought a house and couldn't afford to do that. And I actually didn't really want that dream anymore, I didn't need it. I wanted to do something a bit different but just as memorable, but most importantly, affordable. I had to remind myself that it wasn't about the wedding day but the marriage that happens after it. Oftentimes couples put too much emphasis on a few hours and get caught up in the 'show.' I didn't want us to go into debt to pay for a wedding, we just wanted to get married. Ray and I both loved to travel and wanted to incorporate that love into our wedding somehow. It was risky because we'd be doing everything site unseen and had to trust that it would all work out. We also knew that it meant we'd likely have low attendance, regardless of how much notice we gave people.

At the end of the day, it was about what we wanted. Ultimately, what I wanted. Ray was game for anything, thankfully. He told me he didn't want me to have any regrets. We considered St. John, USVI because it was one of our favorite travel destinations; however, it was just as expensive as doing a traditional wedding in New Orleans with all the bells and whistles (if not a tad bit more). So, I had to find somewhere else.

Luckily, I learned of a beautiful five star, all-inclusive resort in Riviera Maya. We'd never been to that location together and their wedding package was an unbelievable deal. I was assigned a wedding planner and they literally took care of everything I requested. It really couldn't have been easier to do. There was one catch. If I wanted an official ceremony, we had to do blood tests and all of the official documents and ceremony had to be in Spanish. That was not going to work for obvious reasons. We opted to do the civil ceremony which meant that we would still have to do an official ceremony in the states.

We decided to go to the justice of the peace two weeks before our wedding in Mexico. He wore a suit and I, a white cocktail dress. On Thursday, October 13, 2011, we became Mr. and Mrs. Raynard Harris. As we stood before the judge, I remember us attempting to recite the Lord's Prayer and fumbling through it out of nervousness. Afterward, we commemorated the day with lunch at Olive Garden and a photograph taken in our living room. Then, we went back to work. We told no one but our parents. To everyone else, we were getting married on October 29, 2011.

We were one day from departing for Mexico and Hurricane Rina hit the Riviera Maya area. The hotel where we were hosting our wedding took a direct hit. I was out of my mind, hysterical. Luckily, the hotel wasn't severely damaged and they were still able to host us but not on our original date. Everything had to be pushed back two days. Well, that worked fine for us but not for all of our guests.

Our already small group of 31 was now an even smaller group of 24. Thankfully, our parents, most of our immediate family and closest friends were still able to manage it. My maid of honor, Melissa, was already on location when the hurricane hit and couldn't extend her trip. I was relieved to learn that she was ok but I was heartbroken. I felt terrible that she rode through the storm there, spent all of that money and worse that I didn't even get to see her before she left.

We had Ray's daughter, Janai, step in for her at the last minute. You would not believe that Ray found her a bridesmaid dress in her size and in our wedding color of Persimmon for around $20, the day before we left Atlanta. What are the odds? I swear that man never ceases to amaze me.

The resort, Azul Sensatori, was everything we could have hoped for. The resort grounds were impeccably maintained and the guest rooms were phenomenal, with in-room jacuzzis and swim up suites. The extensive dining options and bars were exceptional.

The first night we hosted a welcome dinner and the wedding was the following day. I was swept away to get hair and makeup done and Ray was in his hospitality suite with the guys. We were set for an early afternoon beach ceremony and reception. Little did I know that the wedding planner had been trying to reach me because there was rain in the forecast. Unbeknownst to me, Ray made the decision to keep the ceremony on the beach and move the reception indoors. Thank God. When I tell you that the minute we walked back down the aisle, the sky opened up with a torrential downpour. You can see the clouds looming (and Ray's worried face) in all of our pictures. I seemed to have chosen the longest poems and scripture readings LOL!! It was an absolutely beautiful ceremony, if I do say so myself. I couldn't have been more satisfied with how it turned out.

Allyson Harris

The reception was straight bananas! I was thankful that we'd moved it indoors because EVERYBODY cut a damn fool…. I cannot fathom how anyone was able to function the next day. I'll just leave it at that. I like to think of it as the first of many crazy parties together.

When we got back to our honeymoon suite, Ray had arranged for the room to be decorated with rose petals and had the jacuzzi ready and waiting. I was completely surprised. I was touched that he'd had the wherewithal to plan that without my knowing. It was truly a magical night.

All guests stayed a minimum of four days and enjoyed their own little vacation. This was my dad's first time on an airplane and leaving the country. I was so afraid that he wouldn't come. Neither of my parents had passports when we first told them of our decision to have a destination wedding. I was fearful that he would object not just because of his fear of flying but also because I knew they were living on a fixed budget and really couldn't afford the trip. I honestly couldn't afford to foot the bill for them either. But my mom came through with the clutch and had been saving her coins honey! I was so happy to have them there to share in that experience with us. To have him walk me down the aisle and share in the father-daughter dance with me is something I'll hold in my heart forever. My dad was not well and we didn't know at the time that he would no longer be with us just seven months later. He had the time of his life. His best friend was able to make the trip as well. It was truly a blessing and I'll always be thankful for it.

When all was said and done, the entire seven night vacation, inclusive of ceremony, reception, airfare, etc., cost us $7,000. I believe we created memories that will last a lifetime for all that attended. If I had it all to do again, I would do it the same way without hesitation (maybe just not during hurricane season!). When we left we knew we would return. We've committed to go back for our 10th anniversary and possibly renew our vows.

Allyson Harris

Great Expectations

Transitioning from being single to being a married woman certainly has its challenges. When I got married, all of my friends were single. Every single one. While Ray and I lived together before we got married, I felt as if something had shifted after we got married. It could have been completely made up in my head. But I was more cognizant of how much time I spent away from home, how much money I was spending. Would I want my husband hanging out every weekend, coming home at all hours of the night? Drunk? Um, no. Would I want my husband spending all of his expendable cash (and maybe not so expendable cash) on shopping, dining out and drinking with his friends when that money could be applied towards paying down more debt, putting money into savings, remodeling the house, taking family vacations? Probably not. If I had a biological child, would it be ok for me to be gone all day and night? Not likely.

My priorities had to shift, in my mind I wasn't acting like I was a married woman. Did I still go out with my friends and feed my shopping habit? Yes. I just started to do it a lot less frequently and was more mindful that I wasn't a single girl anymore.

I would get the eye rolls and sarcastic comments when I said I couldn't do something or needed to leave from one of my outings. Was Ray calling or texting me, telling me to come home or telling me I couldn't do something? Not at all. But if I was later than I said I'd be (which was often the case), he would sometimes text me to see what time I'd be coming home, ask me to pick up our son from his mother's house or grab something for dinner. Was he wrong for doing that? No. Most times he didn't text me at all. Sometimes, I'd come home and he'd already prepared dinner.

This was an adjustment for all involved. Ray wanted me to get out of the house just as much as I wanted to get out. He doesn't really care for going to the movie theater. We all know some people can be too disruptive and ruin your movie going experience. He prefers to watch a movie in the privacy of his own home where he can eat and drink what he wants and pause the movie so he can go to the restroom. He's truly happier not going out spending money on food and alcohol and is perfectly content chilling at home. Part of that is due to his being frugal but more of it is due to him liking to be at home. With his work, he's eating out all the time so he prefers a home cooked meal more often than not. Furthermore, we've invested a lot to turn our home into what we wanted and I can't blame him for wanting to enjoy those comforts. I can't help but remember one of our earlier dates, when I suggested we go to a cute little spot in Buckhead for drinks. There was a dj playing and we'd found an area upstairs to sit and take in the scene. He was miserable. We couldn't really talk to each other because the music was too loud and the drinks were mediocre with a hefty price tag. That evening really resonated with me. While we still go out, it's a lot less frequent. Ray is the epitome of a 'homebody' and is perfectly content 'playing outside' (as I like to call it). That's just who he is and I'm fine with that. I'm actually thankful that he's happy being at home. I could be dealing with the reverse situation.

Clearly, Ray was completely unbothered with me hanging out with my friends because it let him off the hook. But he knew I needed time with my friends as well. And sometimes I just needed time to myself. One thing I remember my mom telling me when I was younger was to never have my whole life wrapped up in my husband. I'd made that mistake in the past and didn't intend to repeat it. I needed to be sure I had something for myself.

I had come to the realization that I needed to become adept at splitting my time. Time at work, one-on-one time with our son, one-on-one time with Ray, time with both of them together, time with my friends, time with my family. And I still needed time to myself. There are only so many hours in a day and days in a week. So, before committing to doing anything with my friends or family I would check to see if Ray had something planned or if we had our son that weekend, etc., and plan accordingly. As for myself, whether it was a hair appointment, nail appointment, reading a book, going to the gym, window shopping, watching a movie that only I wanted to see or going for a walk, I made sure to squeeze something in just for me every week. Some weeks saw more me time than others and some saw very little. I needed that time away from everything and everybody to clear my head, reground and refresh myself. It made for a less cranky Ally.

All of this splitting of my time, meant I didn't have as much to spend with my friends and family. I used to try explaining this to them. I don't anymore. If you get it, you get it. If you don't, you don't. I'm not going to apologize or make excuses for being married. Being married means sacrifice and compromise. It's not just about me anymore. Single people tend to not recognize this until they get into a relationship of their own.

There were expectations that we were dealing with as a couple as well. Almost immediately the questions started about us having a kid together. Can we be married for five damn minutes? Jesus. It was utterly exhausting. I will never for the life of me understand why people think it's ok to ask someone about when they are planning to have a baby. As if the only reason to get married is to have kids. Newsflash: people have babies out of wedlock everyday. Don't need to get married to do that. Is having a baby together somehow solidifying the marriage? Trust me, it's not. Plenty of people have a baby right after they get married or think that having a baby will save their marriage and still end up in divorce. It is absolutely none of your business if and when we are planning to have a baby. If you're looking for small talk, don't. If you must, talk to me about the weather. Regardless of the reasons why a couple doesn't have children together, you don't know what that couple is dealing with. What if they'd lost a baby (or more than one)? What if they were having difficulty conceiving? With your nosey question, disguised as genuine concern, you could unleash a whole set of emotions. Just stop. Don't ask. Mind your damn business. What does having that piece of knowledge do for you, really? As I'm sure you can tell, this is a sore subject for me.

Even though our son had been living with us for a while at that point, now he was my officially my stepson. That didn't change the way I treated him or cared for him. But I noticed that some of my friends and family didn't seem to grasp why I made the effort that I did. It was if I was expected to not do anything with him or for him because he wasn't my biological son. Because I didn't birth him, even though he lives in the same house with me, I should ensure I don't spend any of my own money on him or assist in his child rearing? That's ludicrous. What kind of message would that send to him? I wouldn't want that kind of life for him if he were my biological child and living with a step parent.

After we bought our house and got married, there were also these expectations that we felt were imposed on us regarding our living situation. We had much more house than we needed. While it was move-in ready, it still needed some work to get it where we really wanted it. But we felt that because of the amount of space we had, we were expected to take in certain family members. Honestly, neither of us wanted anybody else living with us. That's just the truth. We were just getting ourselves together. We weren't ready for yet another big change in our lives and relationship. I don't think our relationship would have made it. Of course, if there was a situation that necessitated someone coming to live with us, we would have done it and tried to manage through it. But it wasn't what either of us wanted at the time. As the years have passed and things have become more normalized, we've had extensive conversations about it and made plans to better be able to accommodate someone should the need arise. We're better equipped to handle it now than we were then. We know that doesn't sit well with a lot of people but so be it.

I was once asked if I felt like I was settling by marrying Ray. It doesn't matter who it was or why they felt it was an appropriate question to ask. They are someone that I am close to and should have felt comfortable to ask me that. I'm glad that they asked me. It showed me what they thought about him, and me, for that matter. It also led me to suspect that there were plenty of conversations about this behind my back. Anyone that knew me and how I was living my life would think that Ray and I were not compatible. They would have been right. We truly had very little in common. But more importantly, I was selfish and immature, focused on material things and very short sighted. From the outside looking in, someone who is frugal wouldn't gel well with someone who was spending excessively like me, someone who was 'running the streets' (as my mom would say) like I was. The reality, though, was that I couldn't keep up with that life I was living. I was paying my bills on time but I was honestly living check to check. Trying to flaunt my so-called success for everyone and appease other people when the only person I needed to be concerned with was myself and what I wanted. Ray was the slow down I didn't know I needed. He showed me that there was more to life than eating out, shopping and going to the club. And I liked it! Go figure!

Was I settling because he wasn't wealthy? Well, money can be fleeting. There were guys that I'd dated previously that were seemingly financially stable at the time and are now struggling or have gone through their share of hard times. While it would have been great for him to have been in a better financial position, how could I hold that against him when I wasn't wealthy myself? What about the prospect of building wealth together, teaching and learning from each other? When I recreated my 'list,' I focused on true qualities of the man, not his possessions. I know that if the man has the right mindset and the wherewithal, he can acquire anything, wealth included. While we have admittedly made some poor financial decisions together, Ray has taught me how to be more responsible with my money, less impulsive, make more informed purchasing decisions and search for the best price. He has opened my eyes to smarter residual income streams and shown me how to run a successful online business. We've both read Dave Ramsey's *Total Money Makeover* for guidance. So, I'm not concerned about our wealth potential as a couple.

Allyson Harris

    Was I settling because he had kids and I said I didn't want to date someone with kids? At my age, it was becoming more and more unlikely that a guy wouldn't have kids. But, I'd dated several guys in the years before Ray that didn't have kids. It wasn't completely impossible to find. But here's the thing, if I had kids, would I want someone to completely disregard me because of that? No. Is that what I was doing? Yes. What kind of person did that make me? My mom used to say, you can't help who you fall in love with. Do I think our relationship would be different if he didn't have kids? Of course! Who knows how our relationship would have evolved. I think that because of the kid element, I got to see another side of Ray, who he truly was. Something I may not have seen otherwise. And while I don't always agree with everything he does as it relates to his raising of his kids, who says that I have to? I've learned a lot about what it means to raise kids by watching him. About making difficult choices, sacrifice and putting someone else's needs before your own, about giving your last — whether it be your money, time or energy. And I got to see a different side of me. It gave me an opportunity to focus on someone other than myself for a change. I think that probably contributed to more of my growth than I feel comfortable admitting.

    I know a lot of you reading this may disagree with my thinking on this. You may think that I settled. That is 100% ok. You're entitled to your opinion and please know that it doesn't matter in the least to me. You choose to live your life your way and I have chosen mine.

So, no, I do not feel like I settled for less because I chose to marry Ray. I believe, with everything in me, that if I had not responded to Ray's instant message that day that I would have missed out on the love and time of my life.

Did I have expectations for him after we got married? I think that because we'd lived together before marriage, we'd worked through the questions on how we'd handle some financial matters or what our roles would be in the house. I didn't think that would change just because we'd gotten married. I think the expectations I had for him were regarding how I felt he should address certain issues involving our son now that we were married.

Allyson Harris

Growing Up

After we got married, we immediately went to court to petition for legal joint custody. Up until then, there was just an agreement in an email or text, something unofficial. And it wasn't being adhered to. We needed to get some structure around visitation for our son's benefit and ours. We needed to cut out the drama. The previous year had been a nightmare of randomness and inconsistency that made it virtually impossible to establish a routine. Everything we did required careful planning and orchestration always with an underlying fear of our plans being foiled.

The new schedule left a lot to be desired. In theory, it would work because now there was a legal agreement for us to follow. In reality, the agreement is worthless if it's not adhered to when convenient for one person. In my humble opinion, it honestly wasn't in our son's best interest. One could argue he should spend equal time with both sets of parents but this new schedule had us splitting custody in the middle of the week. There were too many issues to count — clothes and shoes, books and homework, toys, etc., left at the wrong house, late pick ups and last minute requests to deviate from the schedule. Besides all of that, he didn't adjust well to it. Poor thing often forgot where he was supposed to be.

Aside from those issues, we were dealing with our son acting differently when he came back from his mother's house. He was becoming more defiant towards me and began pushing me away. He was getting accustomed to eating certain things, being able to do and not do certain things when he was with her. This was surely causing frustration and unnecessary altercations. We were not going to run our house based on how she ran hers. We had to do what worked for us.

As you can probably imagine, our first couple of years of marriage were quite tumultuous. On one hand, we were thankful for the new split schedule because it afforded us some alone time but our social life as a couple was still forced. All of the other issues that came along with that split schedule caused a strain on our relationship. We were at each other's throats, arguing about every damn thing. Just angry at the world. Tired. Frustrated. Complaining about the smallest of things. I felt like all I did was complain. Whenever he said something or did something I didn't like, he surely knew it. He got attitude from me constantly. And he was no different. We'd had a fight in front of our friends and we would argue in front of our son. And we would say mean and nasty things to each other, certainly not fighting fair. We weren't setting a good example for him or giving him a good representation of what a marriage was supposed to be like.

I was struggling with my role as 'stepmom.' Does what I think or want truly matter when it comes to our son, in the grand scheme of things? Will I always be overruled? I did feel that way. Was that the case? Not likely. Truth is, I had tunnel vision about this whole situation. I tried to look at everything from a position of logic and reason. This is what should be done (whatever it was at the time), so why isn't it being done? Ray often had to tell me that everyone doesn't think or approach things the way that I do. Well honey, I. DON'T. DO. DRAMA. I do not live in a space of negativity. I will quickly remove myself from the situation. All of the parenting issues caused me to put up a wall. Ok, if that's how you're going to handle this, then I'm washing my hands of the entire situation. That's your son. What you say goes. You pick him up. You drop him off. You pay for this and that. I know, I know, admirable, really mature behavior.

Ray had a different approach to handling the issues we were experiencing with visitation and custody. What I saw as a refusal to deal with issues and his being taken advantage of was actually more of him biding his time, keeping track of it all, not being drug into the mud and playing the long game strategy. What I hadn't realized was he'd employed advice that I'd previously given him in a different, unrelated situation— you can't control what people do, you can only control how you respond to it. You see, he'd realized that there was not much we could do if our son's mother decided not to hold up her end of the bargain. I'm sure she knew that there were no real consequences to her actions. Sure, we could whine and bitch and complain, keep running to court, but where did that get us? It honestly wouldn't help the situation or change it. It simply wasn't worth the strain of going back and forth. When the time was right, we would take the right steps to address it. Regardless of the reasons behind all of the issues, what was important was to make sure our son felt as little of that stress as possible. It wasn't always easy. He began to speak out about split schedules and having to go to his mother's house. We couldn't tell him he didn't have to go. We also had to be careful with advising him to talk to his mother about it. We knew that would get twisted into 'my dad told me to tell you,' etc.

It took a while for me to come around to his approach. I was angry. This is something I admittedly still struggle with from time to time.

I also talked negatively about my relationship to my family and friends. Incessantly. I needed somebody to co-sign on my misery. I didn't think about how they would look at Ray going forward or, better yet, what they would gossip about to someone else. I'd made a critical error by not listening to my mother's advice about not telling people your business and keeping your friends out of your marriage.

Nevertheless, it all had to stop. I didn't like living like that. Our marriage surely wasn't going to last if we kept on that track. We were clearly not in a good place.

I found myself waiting for him to do something nice or say something positive. Was I giving him something to be nice about? Not at all. I'm sure he was looking for the same from me. If I'm waiting for him to 'act right' and he's waiting for me to 'act right,' we were both in a losing game. Something had to give.

I had to go back to my teachings from *The Secret*. Was he doing everything wrong? No, but I'm sure he felt that way based on how I was acting towards him. Had I acknowledged what he was doing right and thanked and praised him for it? Nope. I remembered that *The Secret* taught me that if I expected bad things, that's exactly what I'd get.

If I continuously spoke negatively about him, I was willing that negativity into my life. If I gave him attitude when I spoke to him, I would surely get it right back. Conversely, if I thanked him and acknowledged what I saw him doing right, I would see more of that. If I caught myself before speaking with a raised voice, nasty tone or quip with a sly comment and instead chose to speak differently, calmly, I would see the same from him. Could that be that hard to do? Oh my GOD, yes!

But I had to grow up. If I wanted my marriage to work, and I did, I had to make some changes. He was still the same person, I was still the same person. I was still in love with him. What had changed were the circumstances. We were being tested. Well, I wasn't going to fail. If our marriage was going to end, it was not going to be from MY lack of trying. I knew I had to do everything in MY power to make our marriage work. If ultimately our marriage did fail, I would know that I did what I was supposed to do, that I had given all that I had.

So, I sought out help. I started going to church religiously. He wasn't going with me. While the message was generally always good, I often left feeling that it was validating my negative feelings about him and not giving me hope about us. I was hearing what I wanted to hear, not what I needed to hear. I still believe in God. I still pray multiple times a day, about any and everything. I just needed to seek help somewhere else.

I started following different social media groups that were marriage focused — Fierce Marriages, Marriage Works, Marriage is Beautiful, One Extraordinary Marriage, etc. There are far too many to name. I simply put myself amongst others that wanted the same thing. I read all the articles, posts and memes. I shared everything with my followers (I'm sure they loved it lol). These groups were saying most of things I'd learned about in *The Secret* but specifically focused on marriage. They were blunt and in your face about your role in your marriage and protecting it. It was a bit of a wake up call and I needed that type of reinforcement.

I also read *The Happy Wives Club* and *Common Sense Conversations for Couples*. I typically don't subscribe to self-help books but I had to give it a try for the sake of my marriage. These books echoed what I'd been reading in my social media groups and in *The Secret*. The keys to a successful marriage were communication, commitment, trust and positivity.

I started actively checking myself in our conversations. Before saying something that I knew would start an argument or responding to something snotty that he'd said, I would take a breath and think about how best to respond to not further escalate the situation. I started openly thanking him for something small that he'd done, any and everything. I started publicly praising him to my friends and on social media. I made a conscious effort to refrain from speaking negatively about him to my friends and family. I know people were looking at me like I had three eyes.

I made more of an effort in the kitchen. I am admittedly not the best cook. But we honestly couldn't afford to eat out all the time, whether it was due to financial or health reasons. He was at work all day and I was at home most of the time. So, I committed to cooking three to four times a week. It was a start. With our son being involved in rec sports, it was a necessary evil. We had already grown tired of eating fast food three nights a week. Pinterest and the crock pot became my best friends. I still stick pretty close to this routine (and now Ray cooks a few meals as well).

He was taking care of the outside and fixing things that needed fixing in the house. So, I made more of an effort to take better care of the inside. I started to buy things and have them monogrammed with our wedding date and name as constant reminders of our commitment. I also made every effort to surprise my husband with the most awesome gifts I could manage. I'd listened to the things he said he'd always wanted or wanted to do and filed them away. When the opportunity presented itself for me to get something he'd mentioned, I did it. Without hesitation. I wanted him to feel special and know that I'd been paying attention.

Anyone who was in my life at this time can attest to me doing all of this. They probably thought I was crazy or being fake, putting on appearances. I honestly don't care. I was treating him the way I wanted him to treat me — just practicing the 'Golden Rule.' What's so wrong with being thankful for something my husband has done and acknowledging him for it? If he feels more appreciated he is more apt to do it again. What's so wrong with not giving an attitude or yelling at him whenever he says something to me? Absolutely nothing. Please tell me how behaving in that manner was helping the situation? It wasn't! It's not mature behavior. It didn't make me feel better. I was mad all the time. The tension was suffocating.

Am I telling you that I didn't speak up when I was hurt by something he said or did? Hell no. One thing I'm not is a doormat. What I am telling you is that how I responded to things changed and what I chose to bitch about, changed. Everything didn't warrant an argument or an attitude.

I also fixed my attitude when it came to our son. I reminded myself that if I'd had a child from a previous relationship, would I want my spouse to act the way I was? I wouldn't want my child to feel like a stepchild. Would I even want to be with a spouse that behaved like that? Definitely not. So, I stopped being a brat. This is still a challenge for me. Not how I treat him but how I feel about what is being done (or not done) for him. I do feel that some things are taken for granted and abused. I have to look past a lot and consider what is truly best for our son. I knew that marrying someone with a child was going to have its challenges. I couldn't just throw in the towel because I didn't like said challenges.

Change didn't happen overnight but things were indeed changing for the better. It took a little time. But I was genuinely less stressed. There was less tension between us. I did start to notice all that he was doing. Maybe he'd started doing more as a result of my actions or maybe he was doing the same as before. I can't say. But we were being kinder to each other. He started bringing flowers home for no reason. We were having sex more frequently. We were having conversations instead of arguments. He started cooking, a lot. He started making a conscious effort to spend alone time with me. Our overall family time increased. I saw softness in his eyes again.

Allyson Harris

The last few years saw us living our best lives. We were jet setting, having a blast. Going wherever we could, whenever we could find the time and money. We have gone to some pretty awesome locations for vacation or to catch a festival or concert. He's personally seen to it that I've seen just about all of my favorite musical artists or theatre shows. We've traveled to Jamaica, The Virgin Islands, Costa Rica, Dominican Republic, Cuba, The Bahamas, Hawaii, Alaska and all over the continental states. We've spoiled each other with ridiculous gifts, him more so than me. He's become a pro at it. We've created some irreplaceable memories. We've agreed to taper that behavior some. We've both recognized the need to be more disciplined in our spending in favor of prioritizing other short and long term needs. But also, it was getting out of hand. It was like we were trying to outdo the other with the gifts. It just wasn't necessary. We didn't need to do that to prove our love to each other.

It hasn't been all rainbows and roses. We've seen each other through failed new business ventures, unimaginable family tragedy and loss, unbelievable work stresses and numerous health issues. But we came out on the other side, together, stronger and wiser.

We've grown protective of our time together and tightened our circle of friends. Trust me when I tell you that you need marriage minded friends in your circle. People who are committed to their marriage. If you want to know why I think this, it's because I'm reminded of the biblical concept I read a long time ago that said, "show me your friends and I'll show you your future." If you want positivity in your marriage, surround yourself with others who have it. Conversely, if you're only surrounded by people who spout negativity about their marriage, you'll most likely find yourself in the same boat. My mom used to say all the time, 'misery loves company.' Sometimes your friends will be all too comfortable listening to you bitch about your marriage and all too willing to give you bad advice. I, too, have been guilty of this, all in the guise of trying to be a good friend. I try to be more cognizant of it now. I strongly believe that you need people around you that will encourage you to work through your frustrations and fight for your marriage. Not to encourage you to endure abuse, but willing to have the tough conversations with you. Able to remind you why you married your spouse in the first place. To tell you what you need to hear, not what you want to hear. All of your 'friends' won't be able to do that.

There are so many things I wish I could call a mulligan on. Things I now recognize I should have done or said differently. I constantly agonize over many of them. But I can't change the past. I can only try to not make the same mistakes and if given the opportunity to make something right, take it. I also recognize that I may not be given an opportunity to make amends in some situations. I have to accept that. I recognize that I was being immature, selfish and judgmental about a lot. And I still have my moments where I slip back into some of those old bad behaviors. I'm still a work in progress. But the difference now is, I'm more aware of my faults.

Our Boy

My approach to raising our son has always been one of trying to maintain a delicate balance - one that tried to impart the lessons I took from my childhood while at the same time affording him the opportunities I didn't get. Of course I wanted him to feel loved, first and foremost, but I also wanted him to understand that life has ups and downs and it doesn't revolve around you and your wants and needs. I wanted him to know how it felt to be told no and how to lose with dignity. How it feels to go without. How it feels to work for (and get) something you want. How to clean up after himself. To have compassion. The value of a dollar. I wanted him to learn resourcefulness, how to see the big picture and what it means to care about something other than himself. But I also wanted him to know what it felt like to have the privilege of having access to certain communities, not being ostracized because he didn't have the popular toys, shoes or clothes, to be a winner and play competitive sports. These are the same lessons that I would want my biological child to learn, these are the types of lessons that build character.

He has household chores because we don't have a maid. And he will not grow up thinking it's a woman's responsibility to clean the house. Everyone must contribute to the house in some way and that's his. One day, he will live on his own and nobody wants to be around a man that keeps a nasty house or can't clean up after himself. He also gets an allowance when he completes his chores so he can learn the concept of working, but also because I want him to be able to buy some of the things he wants with his own money and learn how to save up for those things. Also, how to not spend all of his money as soon as he gets it. Additionally, he gets money for his good grades as a reward for his hard work and to incentivize him to keep his grades a priority. These are things that I instituted in the house and Ray supports and reinforces them.

Some would say that I've been hard on him and may not agree with my approach. That's fine. But I do not believe a person with a heightened sense of entitlement will do much good for the world. I don't want to have a hand in raising someone who is selfish and can't see past their own nose to save their life. He is a reflection of me just as much as his father and mother. Whoever may like it or not, my name is on that child.

When our son started middle school, he turned into a completely different kid. Puberty hit him like a freight train. It was like he put this wall up and become increasingly moody and difficult. And all he did was sleep. The answer to every question was 'I don't know.' It seemed like he was now beginning to engage in stupid behavior just for attention. He was being a follower. It was absolutely infuriating. Those were the absolute toughest three years as a parent.

During this time, I also started to feel that there was this growing resentment that he held towards me. Like his view of my role in his life was purely financial. If his mother or father wouldn't buy something he wanted or he needed something at the last minute for school, he would look to me with expectant eyes. I was still spending a lot of time with him and working diligently to plan family time. But we grew apart. The closeness that we had when he was younger was long gone. He began to completely ignore me if I was in the room and would only speak to his dad. He would deliberately avoid asking my permission to do anything in favor of asking his dad, even though I would likely be the one to take him where he wanted to go. I began to have to tell him to do things multiple times and threaten him with punishment in order to get him to do anything. I feel like my favorite saying became, 'you can do this the easy way or the hard way.' I know that some of this had to do with him going through puberty and him 'smelling himself' but I also strongly feel he was trying to show me that I was insignificant and that he didn't see me as having a position of authority in the house. Ray frequently had to say something to him about it.

As he's gotten a bit older, the mood swings have tapered off some but he still says weird things here and there. He made a comment to me once about making sure he didn't have kids until he had enough money. I told him he'd be waiting a long time. He asked me how much it cost to raise a kid, I told him to google it and we had a lengthy discussion about it. He seemed to think that child rearing was all about having the money to buy the kid whatever they wanted. I kindly explained that money is only part of it. Recently, he made a comment about us robbing him of the experience of having siblings. Where would he get something like that? One can make assumptions but I have no idea where this thinking comes from. Does he feel that his mother robbed him as well? He has three siblings and he is in contact with them. But all are ten plus years older than him, so he has essentially been raised as an only child. There's nothing either of us can do about that situation and it's unfortunate that he feels the way he does about that. We can only strive to be the best parents we can be and hope that he gains an understanding and appreciation of that some day.

Earlier in our marriage, I actually seriously considered adopting a boy near his age. I thought he would benefit from having a sibling in the house. Ray and I discussed it briefly once. We didn't really want another child and thus opted against pursuing it. Ultimately, I don't think it would have helped the situation. It would have likely done more harm than good.

Our son is in high school now, playing high school sports, talking to girls and growing like a weed into a young adult. We're having the typical teenage challenges just like everyone else and learning as we go. He's more talkative with us both now and we get to see the sweet kid come out a bit more often. In three and a half years, lord willing, we'll be sending him off to college and releasing him out into the world as (God willing) a fully functioning adult. One that is compassionate, street smart, adventurous, a leader, responsible, open-minded, ambitious and capable. Hopefully having retained all the good that we've tried to impart on him.

As time has passed, Ray and I have become more closely aligned on how we raise him. We've both recognized the need to meet in the middle and present as a united front. We are not overly strict with him. We have given him some boundaries but we do allow him a lot of freedom. We want him to be able to think for himself and make good choices. He's given the opportunity to prove that he can handle the freedom, if he abuses it, it's taken away so he can learn his lesson. And thankfully, we don't have to do a lot of that anymore. He's really not a troublesome kid.

The challenges of split custody remain. That, too, is something that we've become more aligned on how we handle. Our son has become increasingly more vocal about what he wants and it's made things easier to manage. The emotions have been removed from the equation and we no longer feel that we have to speak for him. He can speak on his own behalf.

As nice as it might be to have a similar co-parenting situation as Alicia Keys or Jada Pinkett Smith, the reality is that just doesn't work for everyone. Do we need to have joint holidays and birthdays for co-parenting to work? Is that what it means to put the child first? No, I don't think so. I don't think Ray does either. There has to be more to it than that. I think what's more important is that both sets of parents do their part and respect the other. That's what we focus on. Maybe one day we will be at that point where we can jointly celebrate an occasion but we are no where near being close to being able to do that. Relations have surely improved over the years and I trust and pray that they will continue to do so.

Allyson Harris

The Future..

As we close out our tenth year together as a couple, I've seen both of us grow in a lot of ways. Of course we've aged but more importantly we have grown in maturity together. We're both focused on doing what's important and necessary and trying to be less focused on what I like to call the 'shiny objects.' So much has changed. I'm not sure what he would say he's learned over our time together. He may have a completely different perspective on why our relationship is working.

He is my best friend, my consort, my confidant, my business partner, my lover. I have now found joy in the simple things too — enjoying a drink and cigar on our deck while we listen to old music, shopping for home decor or renovation ideas, planning for our future, watching random tv shows and movies on the couch, enjoying live music and street vendors at a community festival, bird watching in our back yard. I love it when he simply reaches for my hand. Pats me on my butt or rubs one of my breasts in passing. Or when he randomly gestures for a kiss. And when he cooks! It's those type of things that keep the fire going in our marriage. The gifts and the trips help for sure. They bring a smile to my face whenever I think of them, which is often. But it's the simple, little things that happen regularly that stay with me. Those are the things that truly resonate with me.

There is no pet name for me but I do call him 'babe' and I've nicknamed him 'Sweet Baby Ray' in my phone. Sometimes I give him a greeting card or send him random text messages telling him I love him and I appreciate him, thanking him for all he does for our family. I know he needs to hear it, probably more often than I do it. Sometimes I buy a bottle of his favorite liquor or take him to get a cigar. Out of the blue, I'll offer him a back or foot rub or some sexual favor. But he appreciates it most when I prepare him a home cooked meal and have it ready when he gets home from work. I need to be better at doing those type of small things for him, I have a tendency to focus on doing the big things.

I didn't always think to do these things. If you're familiar with the book *The Five Love Languages*, I would say that my love languages are *quality time* and *physical touch* and Ray's are *words of affirmation* and *acts of service*. For the longest, I was treating Ray as if his love languages were the same as mine. And I also believe that, based on our actions, we both thought that maybe each other's love language was *receiving gifts*. Even though we were very appreciative of the gifts we received, over time, I think we both realized that we would rather have love expressed differently. While we both still have work to do when it comes to speaking each other's love language, I think our relationship has grown stronger out of the realization that we each want to be loved in a certain way and we both make an effort to do so. And just so you know, Ray has not read that book and we have not discussed this concept. I've discovered this from paying attention to his actions and words.

I've taken the 'be his peace' mantra to heart. I agree that if he has stress in every other aspect of his life, that I shouldn't add to that. He should enjoy being at home and want to come home. If he doesn't, he'll find somewhere else to go. I've learned not to bombard him with a million questions or problems when he walks in the door and give him a few minutes to come down from the stresses of his day, an opportunity to share how his day went. I need to do better about not texting him while he's at work with things that can wait until he gets home. I also need to get better at finding the right time to start an important conversation as I have a tendency to want to talk about something in the moment regardless of what is happening at the time. I've become adept at not telling him too much at one time because something will get missed. I've grasped that there are some things that he is completely comfortable with me taking the lead on. What I need to get comfortable with is just doing them. One of the greatest lessons I've learned over these last few years is that it's better if I don't tell him *what* to do but make a suggestion on how he should handle something. My mom used to tell me that if you need your husband to do something, he must feel that it's his idea. Right or wrong, it's the truth. I don't think anyone wants to be told what to do. The best way to sum up how I interact with my husband is to say that I act towards him how I want him to act towards me.

Do we still argue? Honestly, not really. There are probably hundreds of different aggravations and frustrations (for example, he has hoarder tendencies, cannot seem to grasp meme culture and refuses to listen to new music, to name a few, but I digress), but we haven't had a 'knock-down, drag-out' fight in quite some time. Knock on wood. Things just don't incite me as much as they used to. But more importantly, we've both learned how to actually talk about something without arguing about it. We've still got work to do in this area but we've come a very long way from where we started.

Is divorce off the table? I've heard of some couples saying that the key to their marriage longevity was that divorce was not an option for them. It was in one of the books I read and said in a lot of the social media groups I follow. I'd love to say that but I won't. I truly hope that it never comes to that but I know that there are some things that neither of us could manage through, there are some deal breakers. I believe we know what those things are for each other. I think that we would be doing ourselves a disservice if we stayed in a marriage for the sake of it when there has been a deal breaking type situation to occur. Life is too short to be miserable or be with someone you don't trust. I will tell you that Ray might disagree with me on this. He once told me that if it came to that, he would move in the basement, but he wasn't leaving. I'm a lot more intolerant than he is, this is something I know I need to work on. Maybe I'll change my thinking on this issue, who knows. No one really knows how they'll deal with a situation until it happens.

That being said, I feel that we are optimistic for the future. We are committed to each other. We are committed to approaching challenges head on, together. We are committed to continuing to try. Whether that be trying to spend time together. Trying to talk maturely through situations. Trying to understand the other's perspective. Trying to be that support (or wake up call) when needed. Trying to build our future.

For me, I'm committed to being grateful to him and for him and reminding myself that I own the success of our marriage just as much as he does. I have to give as much as I get, and more. I cannot become content with how things are because that's when you get lazy. I have to make a choice, a conscious effort to give it my all. Will I get tired sometimes? Probably. And I know that there will be things in the future that challenge us and come close to breaking us. But I have to continue to put my relationship before all else. It's become easier to do this. Because I want to do this.

In thinking about our future, I can't help but compare it to how one takes care of their most precious things. They protect them at all costs, they care for them, they treat them gently. They don't disregard them or mistreat them. They speak positively about them, sometimes even brag. They show them off, wear them proudly. I'm reminded of a meme I saw on Instagram from One Extraordinary Marriage, 'If you want a marriage that looks and feels like the most amazing thing on earth, you need to treat it like it's the most amazing thing on earth.' My marriage is quite easily my most precious thing. I will honor it, protect it, heap praise upon it and remind myself everyday that it is the most amazing marriage on earth.

Allyson Harris

Simply Grateful

I'm so immensely grateful for his willing and able hands that can fix and build things, literally any and everything. The man has talent. I call him the black Bob Vila.

I'm undeniably thankful for his thoughtfulness. He is a master at doing the 'little things' that are actually very big things. He regularly brings me flowers, wine, desserts and candy, apparel, just because he knows I love them. I have him to thank for the majority of my New Orleans Saints paraphernalia.

He plans and executes these elaborate dinners as a special treat but also grills family style ribs and burgers on a regular basis because a girl can't get enough of Sweet Baby Ray's bbq!

I am overwhelmed by his efforts in trying to surprise me with painstakingly planned excursions or events when planning and organization is admittedly not his strong suit.

I am relieved that he is a balance to my parenting style, how he always gives the benefit of the doubt and strives to keep a cool head.

I love how he sincerely makes an effort to carve out quality time just for me, despite how exhausted he is.

How his resourcefulness leads him to research something with which he is unfamiliar and he will teach himself how to do something.

He's taught me frugality and made me a pro at bargain hunting.

That he is willing to oblige me in my need to try new things and go new places.

That he is unwaveringly supportive of the ideas and ventures I want to try, talks through them with me and helps me build my vision. He is truly my biggest fan.

Do you know this man will eat whatever I cook. Praise him!

How he understands my need for freedom and independence and doesn't balk when I need my 'me' time or time with my girlfriends. In fact, he encourages it.

How he is teaching me to curb my need for instant gratification, how to actually ponder a decision and research all options.

How he is not afraid to let me shine.

How he indulges my love of 80s and 90s pop music. This man once planned a surprise trip to include a Taylor Dayne concert.

He takes me out to dance when he knows I'll drink too much and dance my ass off (and he hates dancing).

His love for bird watching, for nature in general, that's developed an appreciation in me.

He's a true good Samaritan.

How he's not afraid of being adventurous in the bedroom.

His green thumb (because Lord knows I can kill a plant) and how he's gotten me interested in gardening and just enjoying being outside.

How he looks out for my friends and family.

How I can count on him to pick me up from anywhere at any time.

How he consults me for my opinion.

How he talks about me to his colleagues. He tells them that he 'married up!'

How he always tries to see the bigger picture and acts in accord with that.

How I have no concerns or qualms about trusting him completely.

That he wants and strives to do the right thing, the right way.

How he trusts me with his son.

That he wants me around.

That he genuinely wants to be a good husband and father and his actions reflect that.

His brain. His laugh. His smile. His lips.

How I know, beyond a shadow of the doubt, he would give me the world if he could.

Allyson Harris

Thank you for reading about my journey. I hope it has inspired you in some way. The idea to write this book came to me because I was looking for something that represented me and how I felt about my marriage. I simply wanted to express gratitude for my relationship (albeit a grandiose gesture). I've always wanted to write a book and felt like my love story may be a good place to start.

May you find the happiness in your marriage!

Allyson Harris

Enjoyed Hitched & Happy?

Please recommend it to your friends and share it on social media.

We encourage you to show your own gratitude for your happy marriage!

Visit our social media pages to secure your very own Hitched & Happy merchandise and celebrate your union!

Follow us on Instagram, Facebook and Twitter for more content.

Facebook: @hitchedandhappy

Instagram: @hitchednhappy

Twitter: @hitchednhappy1

Allyson Harris

References

Byrne, Rhonda. *The Secret.* Hillsboro: Beyond Words, 2006. Print.

Chapman, Gary. *The Five Love Languages : the secret to love that lasts.* Chicago: Northfield Publishing, 1992,1995, 2004, 2010, 2015. Print.